STARTING STRONG NEW

Discover the Most Effective Strategy to Reach People for Christ

CHURCHES

Bill M. Sullivan

NewStart
Kansas City, Missouri

Starting Strong New Churches:
The Most Effective Strategy to Reach People for Christ
by Bill M. Sullivan

Published by NewStart
International Church of the Nazarene
6401 The Paseo
Kansas City, MO 64131

Printed by Nazarene Publishing House
Cover Design: Paul Franitza

AVAILABLE FROM *NewStart*

Individual copies of *Starting Strong New Churches* are available on a complimentary basis by calling the toll-free NewStart product number:

1-888-697-8278
(NWSTART)

Bulk quantities of *Starting Strong New Churches* are available by writing to the NewStart administrative office with the quantity requested and the purpose of the request. Suggested donation: $4.00 per book. Write to NewStart, 6401 The Paseo, Kansas City, MO 64131.

The NewStart E-mail address is:

newstart@nazarene.org

ALSO AVAILABLE through the toll-free product number is the *Starter Kit for Starting Strong New Churches: Ideas for Church Start Leaders,* by Jim Dorsey.

FOR INFORMATION on attending a NewStart-sponsored College of New Church Knowledge or a Regional Assessment Center located on the region of each Nazarene college or university, call the NewStart administrative office at 1-800-306-8294.

CONTENTS

Acknowledgments   7

1 **Why Start New Churches?**   11

2 **Objections to Starting New Churches**   21

3 **A New Strategy**   37

4 **How, When, and Where to Start a New Church**   51

5 **The Leadership Team**   73

Helpful Tools   87

A Checklist for Sponsoring Churches   88

A Checklist for New Church Pastors   91

How to Use This Book in a Small-Group
    Discussion   93

Discussion Suggestions for Each Chapter   96

Additional Resources and Bibliography   100

ACKNOWLEDGMENTS

An amazing camaraderie has sprung up among those involved in starting new churches in the Church of the Nazarene. There are too many friends and colleagues who keep my E-mail address busy to mention each by name. But I do want to note our regional coordinators for NewStart: Dave Hudson, Central (ONU); Phillip Fuller, East Central (MVNC); Dallas Mucci, Eastern (ENC); Larry McKain, North Central (MNU); Craig Rench, Northwest (NNC); Keith Newman, South Central (SNU); Kevin Ulmet, Southeast (TNC); and Jim Dorsey, Southwest (PLNC). Though I can't mention more by name, I'm amazed and gratified by the energy and interest God is giving this effort.

Jim Dorsey, Southwest coordinator and pastor of a highly effective new church start in Rancho Santa Margarita, California, has written the excellent handbook, *Starter Kit for Starting Strong New Churches: Ideas for Church Start Leaders,* and has contributed other resource materials for NewStart. Thanks to Jim for all his hard work and for allowing me to borrow from the materials he has developed for this book.

There are a number of excellent resources that provide keen insights and additional detail on starting a strong new church. I am indebted to the authors of many of these works. I've listed a bibliography at the end of this book that cites a number of these resources. I hope that you will order many of them for further study and preparation.

If you want to grow something to last a season
—plant flowers.

If you want to grow something to last a lifetime
—plant trees.

If you want to grow something to last through eternity
—plant churches.

—Anonymous

1

WHY START NEW CHURCHES?

God is calling His body, the church,
to come off the mountain of our own
comfort zone and enter the valley where
the battle is hot. He wants us to declare
His kingdom to the world. There is
no more effective way to do so than
to start new churches.

—Kevin W. Mannoia
from *Church Planting: The Next Generation*
Light and Life Press

"But you will receive power when the
Holy Spirit comes on you; and you will
be my witnesses in Jerusalem, and in
all Judea and Samaria, and to the
ends of the earth" (Acts 1:8).

"I feel guilty saying this, Pastor, but sometimes it seems like our church is . . . well, I don't know how else to say it—dead!"

"That's an awfully strong statement. There are a lot of good people who love God who are part of this fellowship. What are you talking about?"

"Oh, I know we've got good people. Hey, this is where I met the Lord. People from this church started bringing me to youth group meetings when I was 17. I was a real mess back then. I knew I shouldn't have said anything. I don't mean to be negative."

"No. Really. I want to hear what you're thinking."

"Well, saying the church is dead is definitely too strong a way of putting it. It's just that we haven't really grown for years. Oh, we get a new family who moves to town from time to time, but then we lose about the same number of families from time to time too. When you really think about it, Pastor, I've been a Christian for 10 years now, and I think I'm the newest Christian in the church."

"We have a number of our teens who are young Christians."

"I guess I mean I'm the youngest Christian who didn't grow up in the church."

"I've been here less than two years, Don, so I don't know for sure. But you might be right on that."

"You said you want to know what I'm feeling, Pastor. What I'm feeling is that we've lost our passion for the lost. We don't know how to reach out anymore."

"I'm afraid I have to agree with you, Don. We've had witnessing classes, but there just hasn't been a real enthusiasm."

"Pastor, how do we recapture a capacity to reach out to the world? Like someone reached out to me."

THE MOST EFFECTIVE METHOD OF WINNING people to Christ is something we too seldom attempt —starting new churches.

The Great Commission directed the early Christians to go into all the world. Yet, it is a curious fact that the Early Church was slow in leaving Jerusalem. In fact, they didn't appear to leave willingly. It took a wave of persecution to drive them out!

Isn't that strange? The Great Commission instructed them to take the Good News to the ends of the earth. Why were they so slow to obey?

There is no question of their vibrancy and enthusiasm for the gospel. These people who were reluctant to leave Jerusalem were quite willing to share their material possessions and even lay their lives on the line for their faith.

It was undoubtedly a matter of understanding—yet not really comprehending—the full extent of their assignment.

Perhaps we can understand their response better when we consider that the action of the church today is much like that of the Early Church. We know that there are millions, even billions, of people who have never heard the Good News. We recognize that many of these people are all about us. Yet we do not move out in aggressive evangelism to win them to Christ.

We understand, and yet we don't really comprehend. We know the biblical injunctions. We've taken evangelism training. We've tried method after method seeking to reach people for Christ.

Could it be that we, like the early Christian church, have found a comfort zone we are reluctant to leave? Creating new churches may be the most effective way to reach people for Christ, but it definitely demands that we leave the comfort zone of cherished friends in what we like to call our "home church."

What will it take for us to make such a decision?

Start with Passion

Let's be honest. Starting new churches is not a popular program among the majority of Nazarenes.

We are aware of our many very small churches (nearly 2,000 under 50 members, or 40 percent of U.S.A. churches). We have observed previous unsuccessful attempts to start viable new churches, and our general attitude appears to be, "Why put a pastor and small group of people through such a difficult and discouraging process just to multiply small, anemic churches?" But this does not mean that Nazarenes are unconcerned about mission.

BIBLICAL PREMISES FOR STARTING NEW CHURCHES

◆ God wants the lost found (Luke 19:10)!

◆ The theme of the Bible is the redemption of humanity.

◆ During Jesus' earthly ministry He was eager to take the Good News to all the towns and communities of Palestine (Mark 1:38).

◆ The Great Commission, given by Jesus to His followers, is to make disciples throughout the whole world (Matt. 28:19).

◆ The New Testament occurrences of "all the nations" can also be translated "all the peoples," indicating not just geography but also ethnicity.

◆ Paul's interpretation of "Set apart for me Barnabas and Saul for the work to which I have called them" (Acts 13:2) was obviously starting new churches.

Nazarenes are both mission minded and mission hearted. *Passionately.* We are incredibly responsive to mission causes. If our motivation for starting strong new churches truly is to win people to Christ, then Nazarenes—lay and ministerial alike—must and, I believe, *will* respond with a passion.

That's what this book is about. That's what drives the NewStart strategy of starting new churches: the singular purpose of winning people to Jesus Christ. Beyond denominational expansion or even the growth of the local church, this strategy, first and foremost, is an effort to utilize the most effective method of winning people to Christ. Secondary motivations, however reasonable and justifiable, must not supersede an all-consuming passion to win lost people to Jesus Christ.

What will it take to move us from the comfort zone of a warm and caring church? Nothing less than a passion for the lost.

Why Start New Churches?

Why should we start new churches? What makes this *the* strategy for reaching the lost? If there have been previous attempts to start new churches that have been less than successful, what makes us think we can do better this time?

Our only hope for any type of effective strategy to build God's kingdom begins and ends with a total dependence upon Him. This is, of course, a hallmark of our Holiness theology. When we totally surrender ourselves to God, we are finally in a place where He himself sanctifies us "through and through" (1 Thess. 5:23-24). Our own efforts can never achieve what the gracious activity of God does to transform us as individuals.

Likewise, bigger and better plans and programs

are not sufficient to build God's Church as a body—
that's His work. We are His servants and seek only to
please Him. Since He has given us specific instruc-
tions to take the Good News to the entire world—
beginning where we are—we can trust He will empower us to be effective when we place ourselves in
the center of His will.

Dependence on God is an important reminder of
what really counts, but it still doesn't answer the
question: "Why start new churches?" Why not a new
evangelism notebook instead? Or a state-of-the-art
media campaign?

Scattered throughout this book are "proofs" that
starting new churches is the most effective strategy
for evangelism. Nevertheless, because there seems to
be a built-in resistance to such an approach—call it
the comfort of the comfort zone, a fear of failure, or
any other number of reasons—it's imperative that we
focus on this theme of passion for the lost.

The most obvious reason for starting new churches
is to take the gospel wherever people live. This is a geographical task. It is easy to understand. If there is a
cultural group of people in a place who have never
heard the gospel, then we can all understand the ratio-
nale for sending someone to preach the Good News to
them. Likewise, if there is a town several miles away
that does not have a church, we can understand the
need to start a congregation in that community.

It just makes sense to place a church close enough
to people so they can attend. Yet we have a difficult

time understanding why there should be multiple churches in the same community.

Multiple churches serve as multiple points of entry into the kingdom of God. A growing number of *newer* churches makes it possible to reach the maximum number of people.

No single church can reach everyone. No two churches can reach an entire population. Sizable numbers and types of churches are required in order to evangelize most towns and cities.

Having a multiplicity of churches provides a congregation for various group preferences. This is the cultural task. Immigrants, cultural groups, and other persons having unique interests in common are able to find a church that meets their particular needs.

More important, however, newer churches more often demonstrate the dynamics necessary for effective evangelism to occur. (More will be said about this throughout the book.)

What's Wrong with the Churches We Already Have?

The focus of this book is on pushing us from the comfort zone of our home church in order to reach more people with the good news of Jesus Christ.

Hopefully this doesn't leave you with the impression that I believe our existing churches are miserable failures, with one foot already in the grave.

All our churches must do all they can to win to Christ as many people as possible—and they are doing just that in a variety of traditional and creative ways.

This is no time to drop personal evangelism classes. If you presently take a pie to the home of everyone who visits your church, keep up the great work. I hope you won't disband your Sunday School and tell teachers they don't need to call on their students or plan class activities anymore.

"DOZENS WOULDN'T HAVE BEEN REACHED"

Art Magnuson, pastor of the Plymouth, Michigan, Church of the Nazarene believes in the evangelism potential of starting new churches.

His congregation sponsored a new church in neighboring Chelsea. His associate pastor, Jeff Crowder, became the founding pastor. The Plymouth church raised a large sum of money for the new church's building program, paid Jeff's salary the first year, and released 20 members from their congregation to be core group members.

What was lost? Nothing. The Plymouth church has grown beyond where it was before the new church started, and the Chelsea church has tripled in size. Magnuson reports: "The greatest joy in all of this is to see the Chelsea church reach out to people. There are dozens of people who would not have been reached for Jesus Christ if we hadn't started a new church."

Please don't sell the church van and stop picking up those senior adults from a neighborhood retirement village. If your NYI president has the teen group interacting in ways that are contagious to people both in and out of the church, keep encouraging him or her. Now isn't the time to remove the sign with service times from your front lawn!

Every church can identify superb reasons to feel optimistic about what God is doing in their midst.

What we all must be aware of is that we can extend the boundaries of our evangelistic effectiveness by starting new churches. A church can come much closer to the evangelization of an entire city by starting multiplied churches than by growing one large congregation (though the place and the *importance* of the large church can't be denied).

Are We Sure Starting New Churches Works?

Still, in light of previous unsuccessful attempts to start new churches, what makes us think we can do better at this time? Obviously, the Church of the Nazarene has been very successful at starting new churches, or we wouldn't have more than 5,000 local congregations in North America and more than 10,000 worldwide. But perhaps we've lost some of our historical genius for successful new starts through the years.

So rather than devise a completely new strategy, why not rediscover and revive a strategy that was used in earlier years of the denomination—with tremendous success?

Before we outline this renewed strategy, however, let's make sure we have honestly faced our objections to starting new churches!

2

OBJECTIONS TO STARTING NEW CHURCHES

Our prayers were often with desperation. We sent away over one hundred families in starting churches. Many times we were on our faces before God to replenish our own force of workers. One Sunday evening we bid good-bye to nineteen people leaving to start [another] church; the next Sunday we had nineteen new faces in our morning service.

—W. Thomas Younger
from *Church Growth: State of the Art*
Tyndale House Publishers

"One man gives freely, yet gains even more; another withholds unduly, but comes to poverty" (Prov. 11:24).

"Pastor, you seem different lately. Like a lot is on your mind. Is everything OK?"

"Frankly, Don, a lot is on my mind. That little conversation we had a couple of weeks ago has had me thinking nonstop. I haven't slept well."

"I'm sorry, Pastor. I hope you didn't think I was criticizing you."

"No, I didn't take it that way, Don. But honestly, it still hurt. I've asked myself the same questions you raised: have I lost my passion for the lost? Have I forgotten how to reach out to the world?"

"I don't think so, Pastor. You're super. Everyone knows you have a great heart."

"Thanks for the vote of confidence, Don, but you said it yourself: you are the youngest Christian in our church who didn't grow up in the church. And your conversion happened 10 years ago. Something needs to change."

"What do you have in mind?"

"Since you asked, I guess I'll make you the guinea pig, Don. I haven't said this to anyone else yet, but what I'm really thinking we need to do is sponsor a new church."

"A new church? But Pastor, I think we need to get our church growing first. How can we start a new church without killing our own chances of really making a difference in the community?"

"I think our own church would take off and regain a sense of passion for the lost if we would make the commitment to start a new work for God."

"I just don't know, Pastor. I'm going to have to think on this one."

NOT EVERYONE IS CONVINCED THAT STARTING new churches works.

Perhaps such people have witnessed or been part of a new start that was not successful.

The truth is, as will be pointed out in the next chapter, our denomination does not have a sterling record in starting strong new churches over the past few decades. So undoubtedly there are stories of new starts that have failed. That still doesn't support the prevalent objections and myths floating around.

Maybe you've heard—and embraced—a few of the following:

Myths About Starting New Churches

"We should strengthen our existing churches first."

First, we must be careful about how we judge the spiritual vitality of any church. There are churches that are small numerically, for example, but large in other ways—like giving to mission endeavors, cultivating an atmosphere where young people are called to ministry, and contributing to compassionate ministries, to name a few.

We mustn't get caught up in the worldly point of view that assumes bigger is necessarily better.

But no one would argue that some churches do not exhibit the kind of vital signs that characterize a healthy church. For this reason, many lay and ministerial church leaders have suggested that we must invest in improving the quality of our weaker churches before we extend our reach.

The reality is that there's already a wide variety of programs committed to strengthening existing churches. Yet newer churches are already accounting for about half the conversion and membership growth in the Church of the Nazarene *right now*. Nearly one-half of our new members each year enter through churches that are less than 15 years old (see chart). If our motivation is reaching people for Christ, we can't afford to wait for every church to become more effective.

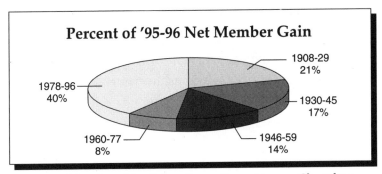

Percent of '95-96 Net Member Gain

1908-29 21%

1930-45 17%

1946-59 14%

1960-77 8%

1978-96 40%

Most Membership Gains Come from Newer Churches

Of course, we want all our churches to grow, but it doesn't make sense to pass up the tremendous opportunities to build God's kingdom all around us while we wait for that to happen. If we did wait for our existing roster of churches to improve the quality of their ministries, there's a good chance we would never start a new church.

That's not a cynical or pessimistic view of our existing churches and the powerful ministries they are undertaking now—and will undertake in the future. History suggests, however, that many local churches have a life span and someday may pass the torch to other local entities.

"A new church will damage our established churches."

One of the most heated arguments against starting new churches is "It will hurt other churches in the general proximity."

Some changes may occur in starting a new congregation, including a temporary dip in membership and attendance to a sponsoring church, but those changes do not need to hurt the existing church long term—nor the building of God's kingdom at any time. When everything is taken into consideration, an existing church will probably be helped far more than it is hindered by helping to sponsor a new church. Involvement in mission often brings new life to an existing congregation.

In case after case, established churches that help start new churches experience the miracle of replenishment—"the next Sunday we had nineteen new faces in our morning service."

When congregations are willing to share their most valuable resources—people—they almost always grow to where they started, and even beyond.

Further proof of this is that when there are multiple Nazarene churches in an area, all of the churches average higher than churches in stand-alone settings. All but one Nazarene church with over 400 people in attendance is located within a cluster of Nazarene churches. Defending exclusive territorial rights is almost always counterproductive.

"But we already have enough churches."
Turn to the religion section of your local newspaper on a Saturday morning over a cup of coffee, and it will appear that there are more than enough churches to meet the needs in your community. Unfortunately, this is not so. Most areas do not have enough churches to hold half the general population. And sadly, most of the existing churches are not effectively reaching out to the unchurched.

No, the number of churches in America is not keeping up with population growth. That means there aren't enough entry points for the unsaved to find—or be found by—a community of believers.

FORGET THE NUMBERS!

Numbers are measures of evangelism, but they are not, in and of themselves, evangelism. Critics of "the numbers game" assert that winning people to Christ, not numerical growth, is the church's true mission.

Antagonism toward an emphasis on numerical growth is so strong that it may be wise to declare, "Forget the numbers! Just win people to Jesus Christ!"

Millions of unchurched people live within walking or short driving distance of existing churches but attend nowhere. Also, there are groups of people with similar characteristics in the community that will not be reached by existing churches.

"But most new churches don't survive."

Most new churches do survive, and in many cases thrive. Almost 90 percent of all new churches started in the '80s by the Church of the Nazarene are active. But no church is guaranteed perpetuity. Less than 30 percent of Nazarene churches started over 75 years ago are still alive today. In fact, we have officially closed more churches in our denominational history than are currently active.

If we start no new churches today, the Church of the Nazarene will cease to exist through attrition. This can be observed in the following chart that shows how our number of active churches has plateaued.

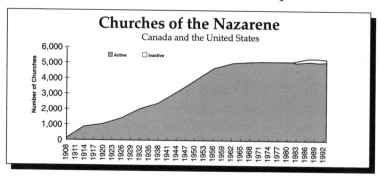

Churches of the Nazarene
Canada and the United States

The Number of Active Churches Has Plateaued

"We have more than enough little churches."

We don't need to start any more small churches, the argument goes. Smaller churches just don't have the resources—people-wise or money-wise—to support the kind of programming people expect and demand today. We would be much better off if we merged several of the small ones together to create larger churches.

Good intention, bad plan. Churches seldom grow through merger. In fact they often decline. Small churches are a fact of life. Remember, small in size does not mean small in ministry. But even if you prefer what a larger church has to offer, don't forget that every large church was once a small church.

"We need evangelism, but that doesn't necessarily mean starting new churches."

Along with Paul, we should attempt to save the lost "by all possible means" (1 Cor. 9:22). However, the New Testament model of evangelism makes no distinction between personal evangelism and starting new

28

churches. The Church of the Nazarene aggressively started new churches from before its official inception through the late '50s, followed by a dramatic 20-year decline in new starts, with only a modest resurgence of new church starts in the late '70s and '80s.

Our denomination's growth rate with attendance and conversion membership is directly tied to our efforts at starting new churches as is seen on the chart below. This phenomenon is not isolated to the Church of the Nazarene either. A multidenominational study covering four decades demonstrated that a downturn in new church development occurred at the same time as a loss in membership (Marler and Hadaway, *Church and Denominational Growth*, Abingdon Press).

Even so, it cannot be said with certainty that starting fewer churches *caused* the drop in denominational membership.

Starting fewer churches might be a *symptom* of an overall loss of evangelistic zeal. In either case, however, we can conclude that when a denomination is actively involved in starting new churches, it is growing in membership as well!

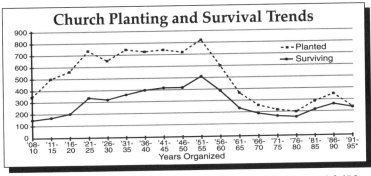

Nazarene Church Planting Trends Changed in the Mid-'50s

"We can't afford to start new churches."

Actually, we cannot afford *not* to start new churches. If we do not start new churches from year to year, the day will come when there will be very few churches at all. And churches that are started the right way become self-supporting churches very quickly. That means new churches produce income rather than deplete it.

Postponing starting a new church until there is sufficient money for the project is similar to postponing a marriage indefinitely until the couple can afford it.

> *The bride bent with age leaned over her cane;*
>> *Her steps uncertain need guiding,*
> *While down the church aisle with a wan, tooth-*
>> *less smile,*
>> *The groom in a wheelchair came gliding.*
> *And who is this elderly couple thus wed?*
>> *You'll find when you've closely explored it*
> *That this is that rare, most conservative pair*
>> *Who waited 'til they could afford it.*
>>>> —Anonymous

"The time isn't right for my church to start a new church now."

When will the time to start a new church be right? When there are no financial problems? When everything is clicking just right in your church?

The factors that cause you to think the time isn't right now will probably always be present.

Let's take time to do the job right, but let's also be careful that fears associated with starting a new church don't put us in a pattern of stalling.

"NewStart doesn't sound very new."

It's true NewStart isn't entirely new. The past offers exceptional models for starting strong new churches. NewStart is a new strategy because it focuses on the singular feature present in new church starts that thrive. That will be discussed in the next chapter.

Pastors Have a Unique Set of Fears

In addition to the previous objections, let's face it, pastors have a unique set of fears about starting new churches. This shouldn't be surprising. Even a totally committed, God-called pastor will naturally have questions that arise in an area that impacts his or her ministry.

Most of the fears will revolve around the issue of effective ministry. What will be lost through starting a new church? Here are a few losses that pastors fear most.

LOSS OF FELLOWSHIP—Pastors fear helping to start a new church will hurt their church when friendships are parted and, perhaps, broken. The exodus of key persons will be demoralizing to the people who remain. They fear it will take years to recover from the disruption of the fellowship.

LOSS OF SIZE—Pastors fear starting a new church will decrease the size of their church. The American culture values size, so their church's and their own community standing will be diminished. Even their district standing might be affected. They may get reclassified to a smaller church size category.

Will denominational leaders think that their church declined because of personal inability?

Even more worrisome than any potential loss of status is the thought that existing ministries that are already stretched to the breaking point will now be impossible to staff.

LOSS OF FINANCES—No pastor claims to suffer from collecting too much money in the offering plate! Pastors fear a new church will lessen the financial strength of their church. Payment of budgets will be more difficult. Funding for local ministries will be restricted. The possibility of hiring additional staff will be delayed, possibly indefinitely. A new building program will be out of the question.

LOSS OF GROWTH POTENTIAL—Pastors fear

A NOTE TO LARGER CHURCHES— AND SMALL CHURCHES THAT WANT TO BE LARGE

Sponsoring new churches is in no way intended to keep smaller churches small or larger churches from growing. The reality is that, if you want to remain or become part of a larger church, you need to be surrounded by a cluster of like-minded churches.

Large churches have an essential role in the overall strategy to reach people for Christ. One of the hallmarks of large churches is that despite their reputation for being cold and impersonal due to their imposing size, they have found ways to care for people on an individual basis. Plus the kind of cutting-edge ministry that takes place in larger churches often becomes a model for other churches to emulate.

Care should be exercised not to discourage congregations that have the desire to become exceptionally large churches. Even those churches should be shown that sponsoring new congregations may very well increase their own growth rate.

that if a new church start they sponsor experiences only limited growth, it will become a millstone around the necks of both pastor and people for years to come, limiting their own ability to grow.

Acknowledging Fears and Objections— a Reality Check

Fact. Only 7 percent of all the new Nazarene churches started during the decade of the '80s grew to the point of economic viability—in other words, self-sustaining.

If this success rate held throughout the '90s, 9 out of 10 new church starts would seldom, if ever, be able to afford a full-time pastor or an adequate building. More important, the hope of someday becoming a

The reason for this incredible phenomenon is that churches have an uncanny ability to replace a loss of members or attendees: *the miracle of replenishment.* I have reviewed the growth pattern of enough churches that have sponsored new starts to confidently conclude: in almost all cases, the sponsoring church grows back to at least where it started, and in many cases, beyond.

Why do 19 new people replace the 19 who left to start a new church? I don't know, and I'm not sure anyone else does for sure either. Nevertheless, once they do, we know that these new people have their own family, friendship, and associate networks, which represent increased evangelistic potential. Churches that sponsor several new churches over a period of years may vastly expand their evangelistic "fishing pools" with the networks of new people who come in to replace those who formed a new church core group.

"full-service" church would be out of the question.

These results from the past decade are obviously unsatisfactory to all of us. So we wonder what went wrong. Were these new congregations initiated for the wrong reasons? At the wrong time? In the wrong place? With inadequate leadership? With the wrong plan? Why should we expect things to be different now?

Honest questions—even the tough ones—are legitimate. However, **the one thing we can't afford to question is the central mission of our church—evangelism.** Reaching people for Christ is the reason the church exists. As has already been depicted in chart form, that is happening best *right now* in our newer churches.

How do we overcome the objections to starting new churches? A new approach is necessary but still isn't adequate. I am convinced that Nazarene laypeople and ministers must respond first to the call of evangelism—not a new program. That means we have to convince—and be convinced—that starting new churches is the most effective means of winning people to Christ. Any sacrifices will be amply rewarded with spiritual victories.

I am certain you are at least open to what I believe is the most urgent need in the Church of the Nazarene today, or you wouldn't have read thus far in the book. There are plenty of other reading materials you could be digesting right now that would better help you prepare for Sunday's sermon, an upcoming Sunday

School lesson, or as a resource for your devotions.

If you're still not convinced of the need to start new churches, I hope you'll give me at least another chapter to convince you that there is a right way to successfully start new churches.

Starting Strong New Churches—the Right Way

If any plan for starting new Churches of the Nazarene in the U.S.A. is to be effective, it must be designed to start new churches *the right way.* This means that new congregations must have a core group comprised of willing and able people. There must be enough financial support to secure and maintain quality pastoral leadership and ministry. A support network must be present to help a fledgling church in its first few years of operation.

How does that happen? Why hasn't that happened in the past few decades in the Church of the Nazarene?

3

A NEW STRATEGY

Someone once said, "It is easier to have babies than to raise the dead." God has already begun to challenge thousands to plant new, vibrant cutting-edge churches for the twenty-first century. He is seeding America with new churches that are teaching the rest of us how to do evangelism and win our contemporary, un-churched culture to Christ in the local church.

—Aubrey Malphurs
from *Planting Growing Churches for the 21st Century*
Baker Book House

"Do you not say, 'Four months more and then the harvest'? I tell you, open your eyes and look at the fields! They are ripe for harvest" (John 4:35).

"I've been thinking a lot about what you said, Pastor."

"Now you're the one who looks as if he's losing sleep."

"Actually, I worked a double shift yesterday. But when I'm awake, you've got me thinking."

"Good. That's the reason I said something to you, Don. So what are you thinking?"

"I do agree with you that if our church would attempt something great for God, like starting a new church, it would probably wake us up. We'd probably start doing a better job of inviting people here. But still, why us? I've not been in the church all my life, but I've been to two or three of the district assemblies now. It seems to me that the district is in a better position to do this. They have the money and all."

"The reality, Don, is that the district doesn't have all the money. In fact, the only money they have is what churches like ours give to them. We're not a rich church by any means, but our people don't hold back on mission-oriented projects. What could be more mission-oriented than starting a new church on the other side of town?"

"That's true. We usually do pretty well in missionary offerings and whatnot."

"Plus, the district office is 130 miles away. Who's in a better position to start a new church in our town than us? Besides, if I know our D.S. as well as I think I do, he'll have other potential sites for new churches on his mind. But who's going to do it? I say right here, it's our local church!"

"I'm not saying I'm 100 percent convinced, but you're making sense. But what's the board going to say?"

"We'll cross that bridge when we come to it. I think our job right now, Don, is to begin praying."

"We'll need it!"

NEWER CHURCHES ARE MORE EFFECTIVE AT winning people to Christ. Why? Good question. Here are just a few answers:

✔ New churches provide multiple geographic and cultural points of entry into the church.

✔ A higher percentage of believers who attend new churches invite unsaved friends to church than do believers from established churches.

✔ When Christians obediently undertake something great for God, like helping to start a new church, they inevitably experience a true outpouring of His Spirit. One result is a renewed spiritual vigor that makes them uncommonly effective at sharing the gospel with those who are lost.

✔ Getting in on the ground floor of a new church is an appealing challenge to even the unchurched. It appeals to the "pioneer spirit" of North Americans. Telemarketing results have demonstrated that unchurched people respond far more readily to the invitation to help start a new church than they do to become involved in an established church.

✔ New churches win more converts, per member and per dollar invested, than older established churches, which means not only are they more evangelistically effective, but also they are more efficient.

If all that is true, our own track record of starting new churches should be stellar. Right?

A Wake-up Call

In 1991 a study was conducted of the 660 new Churches of the Nazarene in the U.S.A. that had been started during the previous decade. We saw that as a denomination we had succeeded in launching an average of 66 new congregations per year in the 1980s. As referenced above, however, the report showed that only 7 percent of those churches achieved "economic viability," even after four years of existence. Even more disturbing was the discovery that the growth of most of our new churches peaked in only four years.

This study was the wake-up call that caused us to begin thinking about a totally new strategy for starting churches.

Our first step was to study those churches that had achieved "economic viability." Three realities jumped out at us. Successful new churches are started with:

- A core group
- Financial support
- Ongoing emotional support from the sponsoring church

Many conclusions can be inferred from these three elements, but nothing is more clear than the fact that

---

SPONSORSHIP CARRIES OBLIGATIONS

◆ EXCELLENCE—A commitment to excellence in starting the new church. The goal is a strong new church, fully organized and fully self-supporting.

◆ LEADERSHIP—A willingness to permanently give leadership and other personnel to form the core group of the new church.

◆ OVERSIGHT—A willingness to provide continuing concern for, and oversight of, the new church project until it is fully organized.

◆ CERTIFIED LEADER—Agreement to work closely with the district superintendent in the selection of a new-church pastor and to choose leadership that has been approved and recommended to begin a new church by a certified Assessment Center.

◆ FINANCE—A willingness to assume financial responsibility for starting the new church and bringing it to fully organized status. However, special care should be given by the new start to establishing the habit of budget payments. Perhaps the new church would volunteer to contribute to each budget of the sponsoring church, even though the district had not assigned the new church a budget. A graduated scale of budget responsibility should be instituted during the years that the new church is under the direction of the sponsoring church.

◆ SELF-SUPPORT—Agreement that the new church will not be returned to the district for responsibility until, and unless, the new church is fully self-supporting.

---

core groups and money almost always come from existing local churches.

Local Church Sponsorship Is the Key

Based on this study and other convincing evidence, the method for starting strong new churches that promises the greatest potential for effectiveness begins with the basic idea of local church sponsorship. In other words, the essential change in our understanding of how to start new churches concerns the point of initiative.

For much of our history, the responsibility for initiating new church starts has largely rested on district agencies and leaders. The Church of the Nazarene has encouraged local church sponsorship by offering *permission* to local churches. Even so, very few churches responded to the offer.

Why should they? Someone else on their district was already responsible for "home missions." Everyone knows the local church has no shortage of existing plans and programs to care for, so why look for another job—especially if that job is already on someone else's "to do" list.

The wake-up call suggested that a "new agency" within the church must be given *primary* responsibility for starting new churches. It is clear that *local churches* must be motivated and *empowered* to start new churches. They must be given the freedom to accomplish the task according to their initiative and style.

Easier said than done! How are we to go about

motivating and empowering the local church to take on yet another ministry?

In the past, we have relied on a denominational goal and reward system as the driving force to provide empowerment. Please don't misunderstand me. There is general agreement that goal setting is important and is an important motivation. It has been practiced in the church for many years.

At the 1972 General Assembly, for example, district superintendents were publicly asked to establish goals for starting new churches. In 1978 the Home Mission Department published a *Total Mobilization* booklet, which listed new church target sites for every U.S.A. and Canadian district. The *3,500 New Churches* booklet is the current example of our goal-setting efforts.

Yet this long-term striving to establish and update goals for starting new churches appears to have produced limited results. Goals have their place, a very important place, but goals alone do not provide sufficient *motivation* to increase the rate of starting new churches.

All follow-up attempts have come short of desired results. Recognition and rewards have for the most part produced disappointing outcomes, though thankfully with some very notable exceptions.

At the risk of redundancy, I must repeat what is for me the key theme of this book. The only appropriate way to energize the pastors and laypersons of our local churches to sponsor a new church is to keep the focus on our mission—*reaching the world for Christ*.

Only then will our congregations passionately embrace a plan for starting new churches—for the right reasons.

NewStart, through various inspirational training resources, serves as a reminder to Nazarenes of that mission. It is designed to provide empowerment to the pastor, the committed layperson, the church board that has captured—or just started to glimpse—a vision to reach the lost for Christ through starting a new church.

THE PARTNER SPONSORSHIP PLAN

Before assuming that the starting of a new church is only for large churches, consider the idea that two or more churches may sponsor a new church start.

A partner-sponsor steering committee for the new church would be formed consisting of the pastor and a lay representative from each of the partner-sponsor churches. The steering committee would give direction to the new church much as the local church board in a full sponsorship church would do. Church members who become part of the core group will be counted in the membership reports of their respective churches.

The District's Role in Starting Strong New Churches

District sponsorship and support will remain a necessary and viable method in the overall strategy for starting new churches. The district will start churches in those areas where no existing church assumes responsibility.

District leadership will continue to cast the vision and keep the need for starting new churches before pastors and laypersons.

In cases where several churches work together to sponsor a new church start, or funds become available to help support new churches in their critical first years, district leadership will play a crucial role in coordinating and prioritizing such activity.

And the many district superintendents, pastors, and laypersons who have experienced the joy and reward of starting new churches personally, who out of their own intense passion for starting new churches, will both formally and informally make up the support network that new churches need to survive and thrive.

The local church working in concert with the district is in the best position to initiate a new church start.

Local Churches Are Closer to the Action

The reality is that, wherever we place responsibility for initiating new church starts, local churches will provide the three elements necessary to successfully start any new church—financial support, a core group, and emotional support by people in the sponsoring church.

It only makes sense that when "ownership" for starting new churches is handed to the local church, it will provide those three elements more effectively.

In a nutshell, the local church is in the best position to initiate a new church start because of:

PROXIMITY—A sponsor church can stay close to the fledgling congregation, providing spiritual and emotional support. A steering committee from the sponsoring church, for example, can invest much more time in the new church than a district-appointed committee, which might be scattered among several churches and over hundreds of additional miles.

FINANCES AND OTHER RESOURCES—A sponsor church can generate financial support in a variety of ways, whereas district resources are primarily budgetary.

When the members of a sponsoring church really get behind a new start, they become a major source of multiplied "soft dollars." They make sure that their "baby" is properly cared for. Soft dollars include cash gifts (outside the normal budget), gifts in kind, discounted purchases, volunteer labor, donated services and equipment, and much more.

MORE PEOPLE GETTING INVOLVED IN MINISTRY—Local church sponsorship gives church members hands-on involvement in mission. This brings excitement and satisfaction to the sponsoring church constituency.

It can better serve as the principal source of the new church core group if it assumes ownership for starting the new church. Then, rather than feeling defeated because they are losing members, the pastor and laity of the sponsoring church get to feel the victory of giving from a sense of abundance.

BETTER TARGETING—Sponsorship also allows the local church to define "the right way" to start a new church. Since the local church is closer to those areas needing new churches, its people are better able to understand the local contextual factors that will influence the development of a new church.

Thus the selection of new church targets by existing churches will be better focused.

Existing church sponsorship of a beginning church is not a new idea. It was the method of choice in the past and is currently experiencing a revival in many churches across North America.

REMOTE SPONSORSHIP

Not all sponsorship must be local. Some churches, for a variety of reasons, may choose to sponsor new churches that are located hundreds of miles away from their own geographic area. In some instances, sponsorship might even be on another district. A church in the Midwest might decide to sponsor a new multicultural church on the West Coast. A church in a declining section of the nation might elect to sponsor a new church in a rapidly growing area.

Remote sponsorship requires the approval of the district superintendent and Advisory Board. If remote sponsorship is on another district, then the approval of both district superintendents is required.

Empowering the Local Congregation— Budgets and Counting

Maybe the thought has crossed your mind: it's not enough for the general church to send a mailing to the congregations of the Church of the Nazarene and in essence say, You have a new job; best wishes!

After much discussion among all levels of leadership within the Church of the Nazarene, including our frontline pastors, a number of significant proposals in the areas of budgets and counting were approved to better enable the local church to sponsor a new church.

REPORTING STATISTICS—The local church can now include the attendance and membership of the new church within their own *official* records and reports until the new church is officially and fully organized. This will better reflect the actual outreach ministry of the church. And the local church determines when the new church should be organized.

BUDGETS—A sponsoring church can now receive the return of the District Home Mission Budget or negotiate with the district superintendent the return of a major percentage of the District Budget in order to help finance a new church.

The various circumstances of particular districts will help determine the percentage of budget returned to sponsoring churches. The budget-return agreement will include Home Mission Budget money paid to the district within each assembly year that the new church is sponsored, up to a maximum of four full years, provided such cash funds are actually invested in the new church.

EXEMPTION—All cash invested in the new church may be reported in Column 11b of a sponsoring church's annual report, which means those dollars will be exempt from budgets.

10% CREDIT—A sponsoring church now receives Ten Percent giving credit for all cash invested in the new church within each assembly year.

My sincere prayer is that these changes will remove most, if not all, barriers to starting a new church and communicate in dollars and cents that the

No. 1 need for the Church of the Nazarene today is to start new churches.

Getting Started

You're convinced? Great! So how and when do you get the ball rolling?

Whether you are a minister or layperson, now is the time to start the process for your local church to start a strong new church.

The best time to plant a new tree was 20 years ago. The next best time is today.

So how, when, and where should the planting of a strong new church happen?

4

HOW, WHEN, AND WHERE TO START A NEW CHURCH

The best time to plant a tree was 20 years ago. The next best time is now.

—Anonymous

"During the night Paul had a vision of a man of Macedonia standing and begging him, 'Come over to Macedonia and help us.' After Paul had seen the vision, we got ready at once to leave for Macedonia, concluding that God had called us to preach the gospel to them" (Acts 16:9-10).

"I have to admit, Pastor, you were amazing. I thought the board would drop the idea like a hot potato. But you were at least able to get a study group formed to work on this idea of starting a new church."

"I'm not amazing, Don. The Lord is amazing. But we're not there yet. I saw an awful lot of blank stares when I presented the idea."

"Yeah, but some people were with us as soon as you had the words out."

"I do believe our prayers went before us into the meeting and made a tremendous difference."

"So when do we start, Pastor?"

"Don, we better slow down."

"You're not getting cold feet, are you, Pastor?"

"Absolutely not! But to tell you the truth, I've never done anything like this myself, and I'm not sure I know exactly what I'm doing. I know that sounds bad coming from your pastor, but it's true. If we're going to do it, let's make sure we do it right."

"I can't argue with that. It's just that ever since you started

talking about how a new church reaches more people for Christ, I've been more excited about my own walk with God than I've been in a long time. I don't know, Pastor. You talked about needing a core group to help start the church. Maybe the Lord is asking me to be one of them."

"Come to think of it, Don, maybe my feet are getting a little cold."

ON YOUR MARK. GET SET. GO!

I confess. I am impatient when it comes to the need for the Church of the Nazarene to start new churches —now. But I'm just as interested—more interested, really—in seeing churches started the right way.

As urgent as the need is—the time to start churches is now—it's imperative that our new churches be started in such a way that they will become self-supporting, thriving centers of ministry. That means pausing long enough to follow all the steps necessary for a successful start-up.

What follows is an overview of starting a new church. It is by no means intended to be exhaustive nor to cover every detail. Please refer to the bibliography page at the end of this book for a list of recommended resources that will walk you through all the specifics of starting a new church.

You should also attend a significant training event as you prayerfully consider starting a new church. A College of New Church Knowledge has been set up on each region of North America by the Church Growth Division, in cooperation with our Nazarene colleges, to provide annual training events.

You will come away from this chapter with the big picture of the kind of commitment required to accomplish something great for God. This is His work and we are His workers.

Keep in mind, the following order of steps—other than the first one—is not set in stone. At times, the steps will happen very sequentially. Much of the time, all the steps may be happening concurrently.

STEP ONE: PRAY

Once the Lord has begun to lay a vision for starting a new church on your heart, the place to begin is prayer. Whether you are the pastor or layperson in a congregation considering sponsorship, a minister feeling a call to start and pastor a new church, a prospective core group member, or a financial supporter of new church starts, now is the time to increase your prayer life.

A special warning is in order: Many of the individuals most likely to be drawn to the adventure of starting a new church might be described as high-energy "doers." Your enthusiasm is welcome—and necessary. Nevertheless, in the flurry of activity surrounding a new church start, don't forget that this is ultimately a spiritual activity that requires spiritual preparation and empowerment each step of the way. Action and reflection must work together.

Consider the oft-preached adage: "Satan will leave those people alone who are content with a status quo of doing little if anything to build God's kingdom; but he ferociously—as well as subtly—attacks those who wish to accomplish something great for God."

Begin right now to pray for God's direction, protection, and blessing.

In addition to increasing your individual prayer time, it is imperative to become part of a prayer fellowship. The most important job for a sponsoring church is to form a prayer group—or groups. All subsequent task forces must bathe themselves in prayer. Once a new church is launched, the same priority on prayer must pervade the core group.

Also, anyone serious about becoming the pastor of a new church should recruit a team of prayer intercessors who will commit themselves to praying for his or her life and ministry. That's the kind of support that is needed to succeed in the frontline, cutting-edge ministry of starting new churches!

Starting a strong new church requires study, sound strategies, and other human endeavors. As important as all those efforts are, however, a successful venture starts first and foremost as a matter of the heart. Without a vision from God and a deep concern to win people to Christ, pastor and lay leadership should not journey into new-church sponsorship. The only way to cultivate that vision is through prayer.

STEP TWO:
PLANT THE SEED AND DISCUSS

You may be ready to start tomorrow—or even today—but this is going to take a team effort. It may take a little while for everyone to join the team!

Layperson, start talking to your pastor about the burden God is putting on your heart. Make sure your pastor has received a copy of this book. Don't use pressure tactics to convince him or her to own the approach immediately. Wrong motives will doom the success of a new church start.

Say something as simple as, "I think we need to consider this approach to evangelism as a church. I'm going to make this a matter of prayer. What's the best way to help our church start thinking in these terms?" Give your pastor time to process the concept of starting a new church before widening the discussion too far.

Pastor, if you're beginning to suspect that this is a venture your church needs to undertake, order additional copies of this book and distribute them to key leaders. A discussion guide can be found in the "Helpful Tools" section at the back of this book.

If you are feeling led to leave the security of your existing church in order to pastor a new church, begin talking to a few trusted friends and advisers before making any type of general announcement. Ask, "Do you think I am suited for this type of ministry?"

Most important, if you are married, you need to discuss this with your spouse. As will be noted in the next chapter, one of the key characteristics of a successful new-church pastor is a family that supports such a move. Work through this book together with your spouse. Don't pressure him or her for a decision.

WHY AMERICA IS A MISSION FIELD

◆ A significant multicultural presence has changed the demographics of America. The predominantly white society has been replaced by a microcosm of the world including all of the world's peoples, languages, and cultures. The United States is rapidly becoming as pluralistic as the world, as culturally diverse as a mission field, and as needy as any other world area to which missionaries are already going.

◆ Society has become secularized, and the viewpoint of rank-and-file Americans is often anti-Christian.

◆ Public life is almost totally devoid of Christian symbols and in-structions.

◆ The English-speaking white church in America has plateaued, and the population is somewhat resistant to evangelism. The multicultural church is growing, and the population is receptive.

As the seed is planted in your congregation, make this a formal agenda item for your church board. Once the item has been officially introduced, set up a "town meeting" to provide information for the entire church and to receive feedback. Some great ideas on when, where, and how to start a new church will result from such an open forum. Anticipate questions —and even opposition. Keep the issue of evangelism before the people.

As soon as possible, initiate discussion with your district superintendent. Seek his or her input into opportunities, locations, funding, and the many other challenges facing this endeavor.

STEP THREE:
IDENTIFY AND STUDY A TARGET AUDIENCE

In one respect it is almost impossible to start a church for the wrong target audience. The reality is that much of America truly is a mission field (see sidebar).

However, stewardship of resources and opportunities means that it is wise to identify the most receptive groups and focus on them.

That principle does not preclude a special calling toward a particular group. When Paul went to Macedonia, it was in response to a direct message from God through a dream. If God has already placed a burden on your heart for a certain group of people, obey His call. If your burden is a more general call to evangelize the lost wherever they might be—hopefully a burden all Christians feel—then follow the suggestions below on determining where the greatest receptivity will be.

Some kind of research is necessary to make this determination. The study does not need to be a highly sophisticated research project, but it does need to be a careful evaluation of whatever data is available. (See the sidebar in this chapter on sources of demographic information.)

Ask plenty of questions centered around the concept of opportunity:

- ✔ What percent of the population(s) under consideration is unchurched?
- ✔ What is the profile of the unchurched within the population(s)?
- ✔ What type of ministries will reach the unchurched in this area? What are their needs and interests?
- ✔ Are there established Christians in this area that would be willing to supplement a core group and help start a new church?
- ✔ What is the current growth rate of this community?
- ✔ What percentage of households have children under the age of 16?

Concerning the question listed above as to whether a community is growing, attendance patterns are not predominantly based on the neighborhood or parish church anymore. The general community, however, will tend to be more responsive if it is growing.

As is the case throughout each step, the heart of the matter comes down to prayerfully discerning to whom God is calling you to minister.

STEP FOUR:
DEVELOP A MISSION STATEMENT, GOALS, AND A PLAN

One of the key challenges all strategic planners face is taking the time to do good planning. It is OK to start the wheels of a new church start in motion and allow the ministry to evolve before every detail is finalized. That kind of flexibility is needed in ministry.

However, you will further the work of the church start and allow yourself the freedom to be truly flexible rather than directionless with a well-thought-through plan. Your plan should be written in a way that anticipates as many aspects of the project as possible.

From a financial standpoint, the better you articulate your plan on paper, the better your chances of receiving grants from various funding sources.

Mission Statement—When writing a plan, start with a mission statement. A mission statement pulls together your strengths, the opportunities and needs you will address, and the essence of what you believe. Now you have the basis to craft a concisely worded statement that defines the purpose of your new church's existence.

Helpful questions to explore as you develop the statement include: Who will you minister to? What are you offering? How will you accomplish the vision?

A strong mission statement tells people why you are here. If you can't tell them what your church is all about in less than 15 words or seconds, you may lose them!

Goals—What do you believe God wants you to accomplish in the first service? The first year? By the fourth year? Write out measurable goals that you can use to chart your progress.

Timetable—Determine a timetable, within reasonable limits, for the development and organization of the new church. Past experience indicates that most new churches reach their potential in the first four years of operation. Make sure your goals are designed to create an immediate impact.

Ministry Approach—How will you fulfill your mission and achieve your goals? High-visibility kids' programs? A specific-need-driven approach like a singles ministry? Refer to the list in Step Five for just a few ideas to assist you in your own brainstorming.

Budget and Cash Flow—The financial realities of starting new churches must be recognized as one of the basic components of any strategy. Advertising, ministry resources, property rental or purchase, and leadership salary are just a few budget items that need accounting. It's not cheap to start a new church.

Before getting discouraged, don't forget—dollars invested in a new church are an investment, not an expense. A new church started the right way will become self-supporting and generate its own income. The churches started by the Church of the Nazarene in the '80s that are self-supporting today began with a core group and significant financial support. When the financial support wasn't provided up front, no money was actually saved. Often those churches have required ongoing infusions of funds from various sources.

Plan a realistic budget that anticipates fully supporting the early days of the church start while gradually weaning it from outside funding.

So there's no escaping the reality that funds for starting new churches will come primarily from sponsoring churches—from you. However, don't shy away from seeking funds and grants from outside sources to help in the first one or two years. Here are a few ideas for funding you can discuss with your district superintendent:

- ✔ **Start-up Grants**—The General Board of the Church of the Nazarene makes a limited number of financial grants available to Canadian and U.S.A. districts that have mission needs they are unable to meet from their own resources. Many districts have established similar budgets.

- ✔ **Alabaster Grants**—The Church Growth Division makes Alabaster funds available for *multicultural* church buildings.

- ✔ **Assets of Disorganized Churches**—Approximately 40 Churches of the Nazarene are closed annually in the U.S.A. In most instances building and properties are involved. Though these churches close and buildings are sold, the assets are the fruit of sacrifice of many people across many years. Thus, these assets are a sacred trust for starting new churches. Districts that funnel the assets of disorganized churches back into new churches potentially provide significant assistance for property purchase to several hundred new churches by the year 2000.

- ✔ **Special Mission Appeals**—Many districts have organized U.S.A. Mission Clubs for raising additional contributions for starting new churches.

Club members are asked to contribute a specified amount one to four times annually, usually when a new church is started. Appeals are separated by at least three months. Most new churches receive the contributions from only one appeal. Occasionally, a new church will merit a second request. Many districts raise significant funds for U.S.A. Mission using some variation of this plan. Even with local church sponsorship of new churches, there is still a great fund-raising potential in mission clubs.

The goal of every new church is to become a fully organized, self-supporting, self-governing, and self-propagating church. *No matter how exciting and urgent the mission of a particular new congregation, unless at some point it ceases to need external infusions of denominational funds, it will ultimately die for lack of support.*

An exception to the goal of self-sufficiency is a ministry directed to economically disadvantaged people who are so impoverished that it is unreasonable to expect them to bear the cost of a traditional church operation.

STEP FIVE:
SELECT AN OUTREACH METHOD

There are many methods that can be used to start new churches. No single method is best. Since situations are different, a variety of approaches is necessary. The following list is not exhaustive, only illustrative. Keep in mind you will probably use a combination of ideas, including ones not listed here. The target group, available pastoral and core group leadership, and other factors will help determine the exact methodologies used.

- ✔ **Advertising and Direct Mail**—Based on the "the law of large numbers," this is an appeal to the felt needs of the unchurched population.

- ✔ **Telemarketing**—Typically 1 percent of the persons called on the telephone can be persuaded to attend an opening service. *The Phone's for You* is an excellent tool for starting new churches.

- ✔ **Door-to-door Visitation**—The face-to-face human appeal is typically supplemented by an attractive brochure, doorknob hanger, or other piece of literature to leave at the home.

- ✔ **High-Visibility Events**—Well-known Christian performers and celebrities are showcased to draw a crowd.

- ✔ **Bible Studies**—One of the most common and successful methods to start building a congregation is through a Bible study targeting certain groups (e.g., women). Some new churches have been started through establishing a Sunday School class.

- ✔ **Backyard Vacation Bible Schools**—A popular approach that focuses on reaching families through their children.

- ✔ **Seminars**—Topics like family and finances are promoted and then presented from a Christian perspective.

✔ **Revival Campaign**—This traditional approach is still successful in many pockets of the country.

STEP SIX: FIND A LOCATION

Jesus said, "Where two or three come together in my name, there am I with them" (Matt. 18:20). While the church doesn't require very many people, it does require a place. This is not necessarily a church building, but it is a specific geographical point.

Once a target area or group has been identified and an overall ministry plan developed, how important toward the success of your venture is the specific site you secure for start-up? Remember the three rules Realtors preach to prospective home buyers: location, location, and location.

✔ The New Testament church met in **homes.** Homes are still an excellent place to begin the nucleus of new churches. Some communities do not permit homes to be used as places of public worship, but as long as the nucleus is small and traffic is not too much of a problem, the municipalities will not usually stop a house church.

✔ Many new churches begin in **a community or apartment clubhouse.** This usually requires a resident of the facility to secure the use of the room. While space is greater, control is less than an individual home provides.

✔ In North America **the public school building** is one of the most popular places to begin a new church. Schools usually have everything a new church needs including auditorium, classrooms, and off-street parking.

✔ **A vacant building or store** is another option for a place to start a new church. Sometimes location is less than desirable, and the space is not configured for use as a church. What it offers is a fixed location and satisfactory internal arrangements of the space. At times it is the only space available and affordable.

✔ Some new churches have secured the use of a **Seventh-Day Adventist Church building** as a meeting place. While the building was constructed as a church, the ownership of another congregation usually precludes much flexibility of use by a renting nucleus.

✔ **A motel conference room** is sometimes used as a meeting place for a new body of believers. The neutrality of the location is one of the chief advantages of such a facility.

✔ **A mortuary chapel** is occasionally used as a meeting place. This is not usually best because many people do not like the atmosphere.

✔ **Restaurant dining rooms** have been used by a few new churches. Accessibility and parking are the chief advantages. Utilization of the space is problematic.

✔ Not infrequently the occasion for beginning a new church is the availability of **a vacant church building.** A district organization may provide such a church building before opening day.

✔ In locations where the weather is mild, **a tent**

or other open-air structure can be used as a meeting place for a new church.

✔ **A mobile home** has sometimes been used as a beginning chapel for a new congregation. Cost and portability are the main advantages of this approach.

✔ **The facilities of another church** are sometimes used. But this requires the new congregation to adjust its meeting time so as not to conflict with the schedule of the host church.

STEP SEVEN: SELECT A LEADER

Next to prayer, the most important decision you make will be the first pastor you select. Conduct this search as carefully as if the person were to become the pastor of the sponsoring church.

The selection process should include consultation with the district superintendent. The right to select the new church pastor is the prerogative of the sponsoring church, with the district superintendent's approval, of course. However, the pastor of the sponsoring church should take advantage of the district superintendent's training and extensive experience in the selection of personnel. The superintendent will always be an important resource person in choosing a new church starter.

Every effort should be exerted to choose a person who has been formally assessed and certified as a church starter. More on the importance of the Assessment Centers for leader development will be noted in the next chapter.

STEP EIGHT: GATHER A CORE GROUP

Won't recruiting a core group from a sponsoring church be divisive and uncomfortable? Won't it create the kind of negative dynamics that damage morale?

WHERE TO FIND INFORMATION ABOUT A TARGET AUDIENCE

◆ U.S. census data
◆ City or county planning commissions
◆ School boards
◆ Public utilities
◆ Local universities
◆ Lending institutions
◆ Chambers of commerce
◆ Radio stations
◆ Public libraries
◆ Real estate firms
◆ Newspapers
◆ Commercial demographic companies

From C. Peter Wagner, *Church Planting for a Greater Harvest*, Regal Books, 1990.

Special Note: The Church Growth Division at Nazarene International Headquarters provides extensive data at no cost to you.

Not necessarily. If the communication is good, this can actually become an incredibly positive experience for your congregation. It will create a buzz around the idea of everyone having a place of ministry. Even the majority who elect not to serve as part of a core group will begin talking about ministry responsibilities in the sponsoring church.

The key person in the recruitment process is the

senior pastor. He or she needs to be secure in a faith that starting a new church is the most effective means of evangelism, and that the work of those sent—no matter how talented and spiritual—will be replenished through others.

One phrase that captures the essence of what is called for is "issuing a hunting license." In other words, the new-church pastor is given permission to talk with anyone in the sponsoring church about the idea of becoming a core group member. That kind of attitude takes confidence from the senior pastor that more new people will be reached by Christ and that God will honor the commitment of the sponsoring church.

STEP NINE:
COMMUNICATION AND CELEBRATION

Exceptional effort should be exercised on the part of everyone involved to regularly, clearly, and fully track and communicate the progress and development of the new church project—like parents and grandparents who keep pictures of their children close at hand in a purse or wallet.

If you sponsor a new congregation, you become a parent. Good parents don't forget their children. The temptation is to launch a new church with great fanfare and then pretend it never happened.

Often the reason is fear that additional members of the sponsoring church will leave to join the new church, but the "miracle of replenishment" will continue to operate beyond the initial commitment. The sponsoring church will be stirred to become more effective at outreach and evangelism as the congregation hears testimonies of how God is building His kingdom.

Continue to communicate and celebrate what is happening in the new church.

Good communication will also remind the members of the sponsoring church that their financial commitment is a wonderful investment in evangelism. If there's a temporary dip in attendance, it will buoy morale as people realize that the net result is growth. Good communication will also protect against divisions in the sponsoring church.

The same principle of communication and celebration should be practiced with the entire district. Statistical reports are not enough. Every effort must be made to publicize the progress of the new church through news stories and other testimonies of God's redeeming work.

Both the new church and the sponsoring church should be properly affirmed. There's no better encouragement for other churches to sponsor a new church.

STEP TEN: ONGOING SUPPORT

It is one thing to start a new church; it is quite another to keep it going and growing. The expense and effort invested in a new church make it worthwhile and essential to follow through with the support and encouragement necessary to keep the church alive and healthy.

The most important follow-through in preserving a new congregation is resourcing the leader. The pastor is the key person in the new church and needs ongoing assistance in developing a full-fledged congregation. Emotional support is the greatest resource that can be provided. The next chapter will provide some specific suggestions on how the sponsoring church can do this.

On Your Mark

On your mark. Get set. Go!

Have you captured a vision for sponsoring a new church? Is it firmly rooted in a desire to win more people for Christ? Are you talking as a church? Most important, are you praying?

We're not quite there yet, however. More needs to be said about the importance of pastoral and lay leadership in starting a new church.

Perhaps you are feeling God's call to pastor a new church or to become a member of the core group. Perhaps you will serve on a task force that helps select a new church's very first pastor.

Read on to discover the qualities needed to successfully embark on the adventure of a new church.

5

THE LEADERSHIP TEAM

At times it felt we were in a high-wire act with no safety nets. Our family left everything we had known in the Midwest — selling the only home we had ever owned and leaving all our family — to go to an area where we knew no one to start a new congregation. We really felt like missionaries. Even though it was only 2,000 miles, it seemed like 20,000.

—Jim Dorsey, Founding Pastor
The Family Church of the Nazarene
Rancho Santa Margarita, California

"But to each one of us grace has been given as Christ apportioned it"
(Eph. 4:7).

"Have you heard the word?"

"What word would that be?"

"About Greg."

"About our youth pastor, Greg?"

"He's the one. Literally. At least I think he is. Greg just got back from an Assessment Center and scored very highly as a candidate to be a successful new-church pastor."

"You mean he's going to be my new pastor? That'd be great. That'd be a real answer to my prayers. When did this all come about?"

"I guess I need to slow down a minute. He's not for sure going to be your new pastor. Besides, I'm still your pastor, and I don't know if you should get that excited about a change."

"Sorry, Pastor. I think you know why I'm excited, though."

"I do, Don. Well anyway, our steering committee needs to vote to extend him a call before anything's official. And since you and Janice are the only couple that has come forward to be part of the core group so far, your feedback will be invaluable. I don't anticipate any problems."

"I can't imagine there being any resistance to Greg either. But when did he start thinking about being a new-church pastor? I'm thrilled, but surprised. I've been friends with him for four years now, and he hasn't said a thing."

"Don, your challenge for our church to regain a passion for the lost has touched the lives of a lot of people. Present company included."

"I didn't do anything, Pastor. I was really just complaining."

"But you touched a nerve in the life of our church. And a lot of people are different. Have you seen how the Clarks have brought two neighbors in the last few weeks? I doubt that they'll be part of the new church, but they are reaching out nonetheless. Greg hasn't said much, but he's been busy processing everything. And as all this discussion and activity has been going on, he's begun to feel a calling to pastor a new church."

"That's incredible. But it almost makes me feel guilty."

"Why is that, Don?"

"What we're doing is supposed to be a sacrifice, but I already feel as if I'm having the time of my life."

CHOOSING THE RIGHT LEADER IS THE KEY TO success in most organizations. New churches are no exception.

This principle doesn't end with the selection of the founding pastor. Since no one person can possibly possess all the energy and skills needed to start a new church by himself or herself, a committed and gifted core group must be recruited to launch a successful ministry.

Even gathering the finest leadership team possible won't be enough. Since starting a new church is expensive, those with the gift of giving are a crucial part of the team.

Even more important is the recognition that starting a new church is a spiritual activity that Satan will fight! Prayer warriors are needed to protect, guide, and empower a successful building of God's kingdom.

One of my personal prayers for our NewStart strategy is that God would lay on the heart of retired Nazarene ministers—and many others—a burden to pray for our new churches.

Where will these human, material, and spiritual resources come from? Local churches like yours! That makes entire congregations essential members of the NewStart leadership team.

Maybe not everything rises and falls on leadership, but the quality of leadership will have a huge impact on the success of starting a new church.

So who will lead the way as a pastor? As a core group member? As a financial supporter? As a prayer partner? Which churches will corporately make a commitment to set an example of pouring themselves into the full process of starting a new church?

Good preparation is essential in all leadership capacities. The sponsoring church's steering committee makes crucial decisions about who to call as the first pastor. Someone needs to join a core group to help with the children's ministry or some other role in the new-church process. Someone else may be feeling called to pastor a new church. So prayerfully consider ways that you can become a leader—or support a leader—in the ministry of starting new churches. Then ask yourself, "Where can God best use me?"

Resources for the New-Church Pastor

"How will we know who to call?" you wonder. Someone else is asking, "How can I best prepare myself to serve as pastor of a brand-new church?" Here are just a few of the resources available to answer both questions:

New-Church Coordinators

A NewStart coordinator is assigned by the Church of the Nazarene in each region of the United States. They are an excellent source of information and insight on all that is available to prepare a founding pastor for the adventure of starting a new church.

They coordinate their efforts with the Regional Assessment Centers located on the region of each of our Nazarene campuses and develop an annual training event called The College of New Church Knowledge.

Within the parameters of their own ministry assignment, they are available for consultation.

Contact the NewStart office at Nazarene Headquarters to obtain the name and contact information for the coordinator in your region.

Your district superintendent must approve the new pastor. But beyond this official capacity, lean heavily on his expertise in both the matter of starting new churches and personnel decisions.

Assessment Centers

The most important decision that will be made regarding the starting of a new church is the selection of the founding pastor, so it is essential that all prospective new-church pastors truly examine such a calling before God and the church.

That's why attending a Regional Assessment Center—and calling only those pastors who have been approved—is so essential to the success of a new church start. An Assessment Center employs a variety of methods—the résumé, references, interviews, testing, simulations, observation, and presentations—to screen potential new-church pastors.

Not every good pastor will be a good church starter. Though receiving a negative assessment can be painful to one who is feeling led toward this kind of ministry, it's infinitely better to discover whether one is cut out for starting new churches at this stage than when in the field.

The emphasis of Assessment Centers is placed on the fact that the process evaluates only *new-church* pastor skills—not pastoral abilities. So a careful distinction is drawn between a person's call to ministry and his or her abilities to be the founding pastor of a new church.

CHARACTERISTICS OF STRONG NEW-CHURCH PASTORS

Finding a person with all of the qualities helpful in starting a new church may be difficult—or impossible. Some provision must be made to encourage the strengths and make up for the weaknesses of the person called to pastor the new church. The pastor need not be omni-competent, but the pastor is all-important.

Dr. C. Peter Wagner lists several characteristics to look for in the new-church pastor:

◆ A committed Christian
◆ A well-adjusted person
◆ A person of faith and vision
◆ A self-starter
◆ A friendly person
◆ An experienced leader
◆ A flexible, adaptable person
◆ A person not easily discouraged
◆ A person who wants to plant a church
◆ A supportive spouse and family

From C. Peter Wagner, *Church Planting for a Greater Harvest,* Regal Books, 1990.

Assessment Centers offer three recommendations:

✔ recommended as a new-church pastor,

✔ deferred for at least two years before reconsideration, or

✔ not recommended as a new-church pastor.

The College of New Church Knowledge Annual Training Seminars

The NewStart regional coordinators work in conjunction with the Church Growth Research and

Resource Centers to sponsor an annual College of New Church Knowledge. A variety of issues are covered, including an issue that is often missing from the minister's course of study—entrepreneurship.

Mentors

Every leader of a new church needs someone to serve as an adviser. A trusted adviser can help the leader maintain perspective on a variety of issues, including homelife, keeping focused on the original goals of the new church, handling adversity, and his or her own spiritual health.

New Church Pastoral Colleagues

One of the most gratifying aspects of being involved in starting new churches is the special camaraderie that develops among new-church pastors. A special network of friendships and peer support is available. There are well-documented cases of sponsoring agencies simultaneously starting several new churches in an area with greater success than individual starts because of the encouragement that the network of new-church pastors provided.

Intercessors

Do you know who is praying for you today? Are you sure someone is? It cannot be overemphasized—the pastor of a new church needs to enlist a small army of intercessors to lift his or her life and ministry before the Lord on a daily basis.

Personal Prayer Life

In our own lives, we must stay tied to the Source of all good gifts. The call to start a new church is literally a call to be sanctified—"set apart for God's exclusive use." Jesus reminds us to take up our cross "daily" (Luke 9:23), and Paul exhorts to offer ourselves as "living sacrifices" (Rom. 12:1).

Part of Jesus' last words to His disciples serve as a wonderful call to the need for a strong daily prayer life: "Remain in me, and I will remain in you. No branch can bear fruit by itself; it must remain in the vine" (John 15:4).

Support from the Sponsoring Church

Encouraging the leader of a new congregation beyond the "sending party" is one of the most important functions of a sponsoring church. The progress of the new work may be slower and more difficult than was initially anticipated. Helping the leader to stay optimistic is essential to the success of the work.

An Outside Perspective

Many new churches do not realize their anticipated potential. A variety of factors combine to restrict the development of the church. Most of these impediments could have been overcome. It is helpful if someone from outside the group watches for danger signs in the development of the new church and attempts to identify corrective measures.

The Core Group

It will be difficult for a person working alone to start a strong new church. There has to be a strong support system.

The core group must include laypersons capable

of providing leadership in such key areas as prayer, visitation, music, training, administration, and finance. Numbers alone do not make an effective core group. Both strong Christlike attitudes and abilities are needed.

There are numerous ways to recruit a core group, but the NewStart plan is based on the idea that a parent church is in the best position to provide leadership through people and dollars. In this model, the size of the core group will depend on the strength of the sponsoring church and the characteristics of the target community.

Who makes a strong core group member? Someone who is capable, available, loyal, responsible, enthusiastic, spiritual, teachable, and who shares the new-church pastor's vision for ministry.

As a target group is established and a ministry approach emerges in the planning process, ask yourself: Is this where God can best use my gifts right now?

Who Else Can Help?

Maybe you aren't called to pastor and aren't in a position to become a core group member. Can you pray? Will you pray? You're needed!

Are there physical resources you can provide to help start a new church? Finances? Office equipment? Well-located property? Food and clothing to support the new-church pastor? Time to make phone calls or write letters? You're needed!

Really, everyone is needed. The strongest new

churches begin with the three things that local churches are in the best position to provide—people, money, and emotional support.

Perhaps your financial gifts will never be large, but you can still support a new church just by displaying the kind of enthusiasm for the project that is contagious. Through your attitude, you can help your church sponsor a new start by being part of a corporate commitment to continue providing reasonable support for the new church for a reasonable period of time.

CHECKLISTS FOR LEADERS

There are several checklists for sponsoring churches and potential pastors at the end of this book. Be sure to take the time to complete these activities as you prayerfully consider ways God is calling you to support the evangelistic ministry of starting new churches.

Ultimately, God judges the way we have lived our lives, not by the level of our success, but by the level of our commitment. What have we done with the grace and blessings He has showered on our lives?

Who else can help? In one way or another, as you are faithful to God—and more important, He is faithful to you—you can!

"Don, you know this is all your fault. If you hadn't challenged me with the fact that our church had lost its passion for the lost, none of this would be happening."

"It's actually a little scary, isn't it?"

"The thought of pastoring this church without you to help out with the teens and serve on the board anymore sure is."

"You know, I've really been feeling as if this is what the Lord wanted me to do, Pastor. Then when Janice felt the same way, I knew for sure we were supposed to help Greg start this church."

"I really do know, Don. And I really do feel good about it. Maybe I'm just a little jealous. But I see great things already happening here—and even greater things ahead. To tell you the truth, I can hardly believe we're losing Greg too. Oops. I keep telling myself not to say 'losing.' I can't believe we're 'sending' Greg too."

"Well, he's going to do a fantastic job."

"I know he will. He was my best youth pastor ever, and he'll bring the same enthusiasm that made the teens love him to your church."

"Actually, it's 'our' new church, Pastor. We wouldn't be here without you, either. You wrote the plan."

"A lot of people wrote the plan, Don."

"Yeah, but you were in the middle of things each step of the way, encouraging and leading. You allowed Greg to invest half of his time in all the details of getting ready to start the new church. You gave him permission to recruit a core group within the church. You even made sure the church paid his way to that training event."

"Don, we only did what was right. And it wasn't just me. It was a lot of people. Even some of the ones who fought the idea hardest have come around. I can't tell you who donated the computer system for the new church, but believe me, you'd be shocked because of the way they were still arguing against starting a new church even a month ago."

"Still, Pastor, I think you're selling yourself short. We are just seven days from our first service. It takes a big person to do all that you've done to make next Sunday a reality."

"Maybe so. But what I know for sure is it takes a big God."

HELPFUL TOOLS

A Checklist for Sponsoring Churches

Is your church ready to sponsor a new church?

Prayerfully work through the following questions, and discuss them among your church leaders:

STEP ONE

Why sponsor a new church?

Is there a sense that God is leading us to sponsor a new church?

1. Are there people our church is not presently reaching that a new church could impact?

2. Do we have agreement from the church's spiritual leaders to consider sponsorship?

3. Are there resources in workers, property, or support we could invest into sponsorship?

4. Has our congregation prayed about this ministry opportunity?

STEP TWO

Who would be helped by this new church?

What community or group of people do we want to reach with this new church?

1. Is our pastor willing to be a sponsoring pastor to this new pastor and church?

2. Are there individuals in our church who may be interested in helping start this new church?

3. Are there other available and capable lay leaders for the sponsoring church?

4. Do we have contacts for a core group from the target group for the new church?

STEP THREE

How would we begin in sponsoring this new church?

Will we allow this new church to grow into its own ministry role?

1. Will we be teachable in equipping ourselves and these new church leaders?

2. Can we trust God to provide for the needs of both churches?

3. Are we willing to release the new leaders and the new congregation into ministry?

4. Can we start in this adventure in faith without having all the answers?

STEP FOUR

What are the essentials for starting this new church?

Will we be willing to pray in and work with the right pastor for starting this new church?

1. Are we able to pray for and release local lay leaders for starting this new church?

2. What are we able to do to assist in locating a place for Sunday worship services?

3. How can we enable the starting church to begin their children's ministries?

4. Are we able to recruit new attendees for this new church? How will we do that best?

STEP FIVE

When will this new church be started?

Will we develop a master plan for sponsoring this new church from the training materials?

1. Are we willing to select and follow the strategies needed for sponsoring this new church?

2. Can we celebrate the victories of this new church with as much joy as our own victories?

3. Do we see this ministry opportunity as sowing seed for a greater spiritual harvest?

4. Will we be able to pray for this new church's success as fervently as for our own church?

Checklist developed by Jim Dorsey

A Checklist for
New Church Pastors

Are you feeling that God may be calling you to start a new church?

Prayerfully work through the following questions:

PRAYER

Are you willing to commit a significant amount of time each day to prayer?

Are you able to enlist a network of prayer partners to support your life and ministry?

Are you willing to establish a habit of small-group prayer?

FAITH

Do you have a rock-solid faith that God is active in your life and in the world?

Are you able to handle disappointments and setbacks with poise and confidence?

Do you feel called by God to start a new church?

PERSONALITY

Are you flexible and able to change in your approach to work and life?

Are you a self-starter?

Are you able to work both independently and with others?

Do you work better in established systems or in emerging situations?

Are you able to handle loneliness?

Are you friendly?

LEADERSHIP

Do you have a personal vision of what God desires to do in a church?

Are you strong at both short-term and long-term planning?

Are you able to communicate a vision and sense of mission?

Do you motivate others to action?

Do you have a mentor?

FAMILY

Is your marriage and other family relationships on solid ground?

Have you thoroughly discussed the full implications of starting a new church with all family members?

Are your spouse and children supportive of starting a new church?

How to Use This Book
in a Small-Group Discussion

Reading this book will undoubtedly be a much more valuable experience if it is studied, discussed, and acted upon with others in a small-group setting.

Small-group discussions are a tremendous place to meet with Jesus Christ—"For where two or three come together in my name, there am I with them" (Matt. 18:20). Here are a few other dynamics you can count on with small-group discussion:

- the satisfaction and bonding that comes with working on a common task,

- a setting where group members can verbalize—rather than internalize—fears and frustrations,

- a place to fine-tune your perspective, and

- the freedom of accountability. When everyone shares thoughts openly, many negative communication patterns are reduced.

Setting the Details

- *Select a leader.* Often the pastor serves as group

leader, but this is not mandatory. The leader should be someone who prepares in advance, is good at facilitating discussion, cares about the issue (but can listen to opposing ideas), and has a good reputation.

- *Determine who needs to be part of this study.* Is it time for the board or a committee of the board to begin officially processing the possibility of sponsoring a new church? Is it too early in the process to make it official and now is the time to meet with only a few select leaders? Is it time to open discussion with a broader leadership base in the church? Work hard to establish who the appropriate target group is, and get the word to those people.

- *Set a schedule.* You can lead in a discussion of this book over the course of five weeks, five months, or a single afternoon. What schedule will best ensure that the right people attend?

- *Involve everyone in discussion.* Adults want to participate in learning settings. Take an active-learning approach to your sessions. An ancient proverb teaches: "Tell me, I forget; show me, I remember; involve me, I understand."

- *Encourage the group to read.* Five 30- to 60-minute sessions will not allow enough time to fully introduce and process the concept of starting a new church. Encourage your group members to read and reflect outside the group setting.

- *Make prayer an important element.* The most important emphasis of NewStart is prayer. Model the importance of prayer in starting a new church by the way you lead prayer in your group meetings.

Discussion Suggestions for Each Chapter

CHAPTER 1

- What percentage of your church has been converted in the past 10 years? 5 years? 1 year?

- What percentage of your church attendees are involved in any form of evangelism?

- How would you rate your church's overall passion for the lost?

- What is your church's most effective entry point to the unchurched of your community? How might you enhance this open door?

- Read aloud the sidebar "Dozens Wouldn't Have Been Reached." Who from your community is not being reached by your church?

- If you were to take a straw ballot on whether your church should help start a new one, how many would be for, and how many against? Why?

CHAPTER 2

- What would the main objections to starting a new church be in your own church? Which are most/least legitimate?

- What are areas of ministry in your church that must be improved? Would starting a strong new church stand in the way of any of those improvements?

- What do you think is the secret of the "miracle of re-plenishment"?

- There are fewer churches per capita now in America than there were at the turn of the century. Why is that such a surprising fact?

- Have you witnessed or been part of the starting of a new church? How effective was this new start? What was done right? Was anything done wrong?

- If the central mission of this local church is evangelism, what are some tangible ways it must change?

CHAPTER 3

- Why are newer churches more effective at evangelism than older churches?

- Why are local churches more effective at starting strong new churches than district or general agencies?

- What will it take to kindle a "passion for the lost" in your church?

- Why is it so important for new churches to become self-supporting?

- On a scale of 1 to 10 (1 is not at all, 10 is very much), how convinced are you right now that your church needs to help start a new church?

- Are there any barriers to your church helping to start a new one that are not listed in this book so far?

CHAPTER 4

- If your church were to begin praying in a concerted way about starting a new church, what are other benefits that would be realized?

- How many people in your church are discussing the idea of starting a new church? How would you characterize the discussion?

- What are ways that your community is a mission field?

- Why can it be said that there is really *no* bad place to start a new church?

- If you had to decide today, how would you start a new church? Where would you start a new church? When would you start a new church?

- Does your church have a mission statement? How well do the ministries and priorities of your church fulfill that mission?

CHAPTER 5

- Why is it so important for a new-church pastor to be approved by an Assessment Center?

- Why is it so important for a sponsoring church to provide ongoing emotional support for a new-church pastor and people?

- What is the main benefit of a mentor in any area of life? Why is this so crucial for a new-church pastor?

- What makes the intercessor so important to starting a new church?

- How can you help start a new church right now?

- What questions do you still have about starting a new church? Can they be answered?

Additional Resources and Bibliography

Brock, Charles. *The Principles and Practice of Indigenous Church Planting.* Nashville: Broadman Press, 1981.

Dorsey, Jim. *Starter Kit for Starting Strong New Churches: Ideas for Church Start Leaders.* Kansas City: NewStart, 1997.

Malphurs, Aubrey. *Planting Growing Churches for the 21st Century.* Grand Rapids: Baker Book House, 1992.

Mannoia, Kevin W. *Church Planting: The Next Generation.* Indianapolis: Light and Life Press, 1994.

Owen, Roy W., ed. *The Pastor's Helper for Growing a New Church.* New Church Growth Department, Home Mission Board, Southern Baptist Convention.

Schaller, Lyle E. *44 Questions for Church Planters.* Nashville: Abingdon Press, 1991.

Wagner, C. Peter. *Church Planting for a Great Harvest.* Ventura, Calif.: Regal Books, 1990.

Warren, Rick. *The Purpose Driven Church: Growth Without Compromising Your Message and Mission.* Grand Rapids: Zondervan Publishing House, 1995.

Order toll-free from the NewStart order number:

1-888-697-8278
(NWSTART)